WAC STATS

The Facts About Women

THE NEW PRESS

New York

The Women's Action Coalition (WAC) is an open alliance of women committed to DIRECT ACTION on issues affecting the rights of all women. We are witnesses to the current economic, cultural, and political pressures that limit women's lives and to the horrifying effect of these limitations. As current legislation fails to reflect the experience of women, we support the immediate enactment of an ERA initiative. WAC insists on economic parity and representation for all women, and an end to homophobia, racism, religious prejudice, and violence against women. We insist on every woman's right to quality health care, child care, and reproductive freedom.

We will exercise our full creative power to launch a visible and remarkable resistance.

WAC IS WATCHING. WE WILL TAKE ACTION.

NOTE FROM THE EDITORS

Our decision to compile a book of statistics is an attempt to expose the realities and inequities confronting women within this culture. It is by no means a comprehensive study but should be considered an in-progress resource book to be used in our continuing fight against discrimination.

The statistics were researched by many women from many sources. If certain areas seem incomplete, it is due, at least in part, to prejudice in our culture which does not safely allow for women to come forward about their sexual identity, violence against them, or discrimination in the workplace.

The first edition of WAC Stats, self-published by the Women's Action Coalition, was compiled during the months leading up to President Clinton's election. The overtly discriminatory policies of the previous administration made a clear target for our anger. Since the 1992 election, the Clinton administration has taken a number of positive steps toward rectifying certain injustices against women. However, donations to socially based organizations have dropped dramatically, and the Christian right has intensified its efforts to abolish the separation of church and state. The danger we face now is in thinking our fight is over!

We would like to thank the following women for their contributions to this publication: Carole Ashley, Joan Beard, Ellen Brooks, Karen Casamassima, P.J. Corso, Peggy Diggs, Pam Elam, Jean Fineberg, Melanie Katzman, Eleanor Kovachevich, Marcy Knopf, Julia Kunin, Margot Lovejoy, Eileen McKeating, Julie Mertus, Catherine Morris, Kathy Parker, Anne R. Pasternak, Sujoya Roy, Ellen Salpeter, Hope Sandrow, Maria Schopp, Jenny Scobel, Jane Sherry, Kim Sykes, Ann Volkes, Andrea Wolper.

We thank our editor at The New Press, David Sternbach, for his patience and enthusiasm, and WAC for its support.

Andrea Blum
Julie Harrison
Barbara Ess
Gail Vachon

Published in the United States by The New Press, New York
Distributed by W. W. Norton & Company, Inc.
500 Fifth Avenue, New York, NY 10110

LIBRARY OF CONGRESS CATALOGING-IN-PUBLICATION DATA

WAC stats : the facts about women / edited by Women's
Action Coalition. — 2nd updated and rev. ed.
    p. cm.
    Includes bibliographical references and index.
    ISBN 1-56584-122-0
    1. Women—United States—Statistics. I. Women's
Action Coalition (New York, N.Y.)
HQ1421.W33 1993
305.4'0973'021—dc20   93-3987

First New Press Edition

Book design by Laura Lindgren

Established in 1990 as a major alternative to the large, commercial publishing houses, The New Press is the first full-scale nonprofit American book publisher outside of the university presses. The Press is operated editorially in the public interest, rather than for private gain; it is committed to publishing in innovative ways works of educational, cultural, and community value, which despite their intellectual merits might not normally be "commercially" viable. The New Press's editorial offices are located at The City University of New York.

Printed in the United States of America.

10 9 8 7 6 5 4 3 2 1

For information about WAC, call (212) 967-7711, ext. WACM (9226)
or write to WAC at:
P.O. Box 1862
Chelsea Station
New York, NY 10011

Printed on recycled paper.

CONTENTS

In 1920, women attained the right to vote.
This was also the first year of the Miss America pageant.

There are approximately 1.6 million abortions in the U.S. each year.[1]

73% of women who have abortions are unmarried; 26% of them are teenagers; 33% of them have incomes under $11,000.[2]

In 1987, 1 in 6 abortion patients described herself as being a "born again or evangelical Christian."[1]

Catholic women are 30% more likely than Protestants to have an abortion.[1]

16,000 women have abortions each year as a result of rape or incest.[1]

55% of teenagers under the age of 18 who obtain an abortion do so with parental consent.[1]

Total public dollars spent for contraceptive services fell by one-third between 1980 and 1990.[1]

40,000 teenage girls drop out of school each year because of pregnancy.[1]

More than 1 million teenage girls become pregnant each year. Public funds pay for one-half of those births.[1]

Maternal mortality rates for mothers under age 15 is 60% greater than for women in their 20s.[1]

Less than 1% of all abortion patients experience a major complication.[1]

The risk of death associated with childbirth is 11 times higher than with an abortion.[1]

For every $1.00 spent by government for abortions for poor women, $4.40 is saved in medical and welfare expenditures for an unintended birth.[1]

An estimated 1.2 million additional unintended pregnancies would occur each year in the absence of publicly funded women's health services.[1]

1 in 5 women, many of whom are women of color, rely on Title X
family-planning clinics. Title X funding was cut 66% between 1980 and
1990.[1]

Before *Roe v. Wade,* 10,000 women died each year in the U.S. from illegal
abortions. 50% of these women were women of color.[1]

The federal government will not fund abortions but continues to pay
90% of the cost of sterilization.[1]

150,000 pregnancies worldwide end in abortion every day. On the average,
1 woman each minute has complications in pregnancy or childbirth.[3]

One-fourth of all women live in countries where abortion is prohibited.[3]

After the parental consent law went into effect in Minnesota, the birth-
rate for 15–17-year-old girls went up 40%.[4]

A CNN/Gallup poll showed that 64% of Americans oppose the potential
overturn of *Roe v. Wade.*[5]

83% of the counties in the U.S. (including 16% of metropolitan areas)
have no identifiable abortion facilities, yet these counties are home to
31% of all women aged 15–44.[6]

RU486, an antiprogesterone drug shown to be 96% effective in termi-
nating pregnancy in the first 9 weeks, is banned for import in the U.S.[10]

One of President Clinton's first acts was to direct the FDA to reassess the
ban on personal-use import of RU486 and to assess initiatives for its
testing, licensing, and manufacturing in the U.S.[6]

A 1991 study found that only 12.4% of American medical schools
routinely teach residents how to perform abortions, down from 22.6% in
1986. Nearly one-third offer no training at all in abortion.[7]

200,000 Third-World women die each year—1 every 3 minutes—as a result of the antiabortion policies of their own governments and the U.S. policy which cut off aid to any organization overseas that advocates or counsels women on the option of abortion.[3,9]

With the *Bray* decision, the Supreme Court denied family-planning clinics federal protection from antichoice blockades and harassment.[9]

Since 1976, the Hyde amendment has banned federal funding for abortions, thus, in effect, allowing women of means to procure abortions but denying this same freedom to poor women. President Clinton has announced his desire to abolish the Hyde amendment.[9]

The Title X "gag rule," introduced by the Reagan administration in 1987, would forbid medical professionals in federally funded clinics from giving out any information about abortion. This was overturned by President Clinton 2 days after he took office.[9]

Every tax dollar spent on providing birth control to women who otherwise might not have access to it saves the taxpayer over $4.[2]

Among married women, sterilization is the most common form of contraception. The woman is the sterilized partner in nearly two-thirds of such couples.[2]

There were 100,000 users of Norplant birth control implants in 1991, the first year it was commercially available, and 500,000 women will have used Norplant by the end of 1992.[12]

Of the 39 million women at risk of unintended pregnancy, 9 in 10, or 35 million, use some sort of contraceptive.[12]

13.4 million women use a reversible contraceptive method like the pill, a diaphragm or an IUD that requires a medical visit.[12]

In the 60s and 70s there were over 2 dozen pharmaceutical companies doing research in birth control. Over the past 20 years, all except Ortho Pharmaceutical Corporation have abandoned this research.[13]

SOURCES

1. *Facts in Brief, Abortion in the United States*, The Alan Guttmacher Institute: New York, 1991.
2. Paula Ries and Anne J. Stone, eds., *The American Woman 1992–93*, New York: W. W. Norton, 1992.
3. World Health Organization, 1992.
4. Susan Faludi, *Backlash*, New York: Crown Publishers, 1991.
5. *Feminist Majority Report*, Summer 1992.
6. S. K. Henshaw et al. "Abortion Services in the U.S.," *Family Planning Perspective* 19 (1987): 63.
7. William J. Clinton, Memorandum published in the *Federal Register*, January 27, 1993.
8. "Abortion Clinics Seek Doctors but Find Few," *New York Times*, March 31, 1993.
9. National Public Radio, "All Things Considered," March 30, 1993.
10. Planned Parenthood of New York City, 1993.
11. "Foundation Presses for RU486 Research," *Feminist Majority Report*, Summer 1992.
12. "Contraceptive Use: Facts and Figures," *New York Times*, December 17, 1992.
13. Baulieu, "The Abortion Pill," *Medical Tribune*, 1992.

In 1992 there were 128,500 women with the HIV virus.[1]

In 1992 there were 24,307 women with AIDS.[1]

It is estimated that 3 million women will die of AIDS during this decade.[5]

Women of color account for 73% of women with AIDS in the U.S.[4]

Worldwide, women accounted for 40% of those infected with HIV in 1992, up from 25% in 1990.[7]

Within 2 years, 1 in every 6 new AIDS cases in the U.S. will be women.[7]

By the end of the decade, as many women as men will be diagnosed with AIDS worldwide.[2]

In 1987, AIDS was the 8th-leading cause of death in women of child-bearing age in the U.S. In 1991, it became the 5th.[8]

There are an estimated 1 million people in the U.S. infected with HIV: 1 in 100 adult males and 1 in 800 adult females.[2]

In New York City, AIDS is the leading killer of women between the ages of 25 and 34.[2]

A study at a shelter for runaway and homeless youth reported that 5% were infected with HIV.[3]

85% of women with AIDS are of reproductive age (15–44 years old).[4]

More than one-third of HIV-infected women anticipated becoming pregnant.[4]

Between 1988 and 1990, teenage AIDS rose 40%.[5]

The rate of unknown causes of HIV infection for women is more than double that of men.[5]

By the year 2000, 40 million women, men, and children worldwide will be infected with the HIV virus.[4]

Between 1989 and 1990, new AIDS cases increased 34% among women and 22% among men.[4]

In the last few years, AIDS cases in the Asian community have doubled every 10 months. The peak age of Asian women with AIDS is 30–49.[4]

Heterosexual transmission outnumbers all other categories by which people acquire the HIV virus and may account for more than 80% of HIV transmission by the end of the decade.[6]

51% of women acquired HIV through use of contaminated equipment for intravenous drug use (IVDU).[4]

IVDUs comprise 21% of all diagnosed people with AIDS in the U.S. One-half of all women with AIDS are IVDUs.[4]

29% of women are infected with HIV through heterosexual contact.[4]

In New York and New Jersey, AIDS is the leading cause of death among African-American women aged 15–44.[4]

57% of women with AIDS and 54% of children with AIDS are African American.[6]

17% of women with AIDS and 21% of children with AIDS are Hispanic.[6]

In a survey of "high-achieving" high school seniors who are sexually active, 38% of them said they never use a condom.[9]

Incidence of AIDS among Latina women is 11 times that of non-Latina women.[4]

Between 1988 and 1991, HIV infection rates among women giving birth in New York City rose by 12% for African-American women but declined by a quarter for white women and by a third for Latina women.[11]

One-third of sexually active teens use contraception; one-fourth of those use condoms.[4]

The average survival time for women diagnosed with AIDS is 5 to 6 months. Women with AIDS die 2 times faster than men with AIDS.[4,10]

The transmission rate of HIV from woman to fetus during pregnancy is approximately 35%.[4]

The 1991 estimated HIV infection rate among 15–49-year-old women was:[6]

Sub-Saharan Africa	2,500,000 cases
North America	128,500
Western Europe	60,000
Eastern Europe	4,000
Australia/New Zealand	4,000
Southern Asia	200,000
North Africa	10,000.

Globally, in 1991, more than 500,000 pediatric AIDS cases resulted from prenatal transmission.[6]

98% of heterosexual transmission of the HIV virus is from men to women; only 2% is from women to men.[12]

SOURCES

1. *AIDS in the World*, Cambridge: Harvard University Press, 1992.
2. Center for Disease Control Commission on AIDS, 1992.
3. Center for Population Option, 1992.
4. ACT UP, eds., *Women, AIDS, and Activism*, Boston: South End Press, 1990.
5. Dr. James Chin, World Health Organization survey, 1992.
6. Dr. King Holmes, Director of Center for AIDS and Sexually Transmitted Disease, Seattle: University of Washington, 1992.
7. "Rose Colored View on AIDS," *Boston Globe*, July 24, 1992.
8. WORLD, The Women's AIDS Group, 1992.
9. WNBC-TV News, May 19, 1992.
10. Pat Closer, VI & VII International Conference on AIDS, 1992.
11. "Unheard Voices: Women with AIDS," Marie St. Cyr-Delpe, *FYI*, New York Foundation for the Arts, Summer 1992.
12. "Women, Get the Facts About AIDS," United for AIDS Action flyer, 1992.

51.2% of all artists in the U.S. are women.[1]

30.7% of all photographers are women.[1]

90% of all artist's models are women.[4]

67% of bachelor degrees in Fine Arts go to women.[3]

46% of bachelor degrees in Photography go to women.[3]

65% of bachelor degrees in Painting go to women.[3]

60% of MFAs in Fine Arts go to women.[3]

55% of MFAs in Painting go to women.[3]

47% of MFAs in Photography go to women.[3]

59% of Ph.D.s in Fine Arts go to women.[3]

66.5% of Ph.D.s in Art History go to women.[2]

59% of trained artists and art historians are women.[2]

33% of art faculty are women.[2]

5% of works in museums are by women.[6]

17% of works in galleries are by women.[2]

26% of artists reviewed in art periodicals are women.[4]

Women artists' income is 30% that of male artists'.[4]

30% of Guggenheim grants go to women.[7]

42% of $5,000 NEA grants go to women.[7]

33% of $10,000 NEA grants go to women.[7]

29% of $15,000 NEA grants go to women.[7]

25% of $25,000 NEA grants go to women.[7]

Of the art commissioned by the Department of Cultural Affairs Percent for Art Program in New York City, 70% have been artists of color, 41% women, 39% of the 41% women of color.[9]

Of the 1992 New York Foundation for the Arts awards given, women received 53.4%, men received 46.6%.[10]

Of the world's top 200 collectors, approximately 128 are male, 52 are male-female couples, and 20 are female.[8]

7 of 36 one-person museum exhibitions in the 1991–92 New York season were by women.[5]

SOURCES

1. 1990 Statistical Abstract of the United States.
2. Eleanor Dickenson, "Gender Discrimination in the Art World," paper prepared for the College Art Association, Coalition of Women, February 15, 1990, New York.
3. U.S. Department of Education, National Center for Education Statistics, 1989–90.
4. Devorah L. Knoff, unpublished manuscript.
5. Art in America 1991–92.
6. Guerrilla Girls poster, New York, 1991.
7. Women's Caucus for Art, Moore College of Art Fact Sheet, citing Rosen & Browes, 1989.
8. Artnews, cover article, January 1992, pp. 79–91.
9. Department of Cultural Affairs, Percent for Art, 1992.
10. New York Foundation for the Arts, 1992.

1 out of 8 women in the U.S. will develop breast cancer in her lifetime—a risk that was 1 out of 14 in 1960.[1,4]

Breast cancer is the most common form of cancer in American women. It occurs rarely in men.[1]

5% of the money spent for cancer research is spent on breast cancer.[5]

Breast cancer is the leading cause of cancer death for African-American women.[1]

This year, breast cancer will be newly diagnosed every 3 minutes, and a woman will die from breast cancer every 12 minutes.[1]

In 1993, 182,000 new cases of female breast cancer will be diagnosed, and 46,000 women will die from the disease.[9]

In this decade, an estimated 2 million women will learn they have breast or cervical cancer, and more than a half-million women are expected to die.[7]

A disproportionate number of the 2 million deaths from breast or cervical cancer will occur among women of low income.[7]

By age 40, the risk of breast cancer is 1 in 217; by age 60 it is 1 in 24; and it does not reach the predicted 1 in 8 until age 95.[8]

The incidence of breast cancer in all races rose 25.8% from 1973 to 1988; the mortality rate rose 1.8% in the same period.[1]

28% of all cancers affecting women is breast cancer; 11% is lung cancer. 20% of cancer deaths among women are from lung cancer; 18% from breast cancer.[2]

In 1987–88, more white women than African-American women were diagnosed with breast cancer, but 32% of African-American women as opposed to 24% of the white women died from it.[2]

Women having children over age 30 are twice as likely to develop breast cancer.[3]

Women over 30 with a family history of breast cancer have a 575% greater risk of developing the disease than do other women.[3]

Breast cancer incidence increases with age, rising sharply after age 40. 80% of all breast cancers occur in women over 50 years of age.[1,4]

The 5-year survival rate for localized breast cancer has risen from 78% in the 1940s to 93% today.[9]

Over 80% of breast lumps are benign.[1]

70% of African-American and Latina women have never had a mammogram.[2]

Recent data indicates that, for women under 50, the risks of having a mammogram may not outweigh the benefits.[6]

Most women who get breast cancer have no identifiable risk factor.[6]

SOURCES

1. National Alliance of Breast Cancer Organizations (NABCO), New York, February 1992, 1993.
2. Paula Ries and Anne J. Stone, eds., *The American Woman 1992–93*, New York: W. W. Norton, 1992.
3. Center for Disease Control, *Medical Tribune*, 1992.
4. "Chance of Breast Cancer is Figured at 1 in 8," *New York Times*, citing the National Cancer Institute, September 27, 1992.
5. "For the Record," *Feminist Majority Report*, September 1992.
6. "Nightline," ABC-TV, March 19, 1993.
7. The National Breast and Cervical Cancer Early Detection Program, U.S. Department of Health and Human Services, Center for Disease Control, 1992–93.
8. National Cancer Institute, 1992 Cancer Statistics Review.
9. "Cancer Facts and Figures—1993," American Cancer Society, Atlanta, GA, 1993.

The amount spent on cosmetics every year could buy:
> 3 times the amount of day care offered by the U.S. government; or
> 2,000 women's health clinics; or
> 75,000 women's film, music, literature, or art festivals; or
> 50 women's universities; or
> 1 million highly paid domestic or child-care workers; or
> 1 million highly paid home-support workers for the housebound elderly; or
> 33,000 battered-women's shelters; or
> 2 billion tubes of contraceptive cream; or
> 200,000 vans for late-night safe transport; or
> 400,000 full four-year university scholarships for women; or
> 20 million airplane tickets around the world.[2]

Cosmetics are a $20-billion industry worldwide.[1]

The cosmetic surgery industry in the U.S. grosses $300 million a year and is growing annually by 10%.[2]

The number of women using cosmetic surgery to alter their bodies has increased 61% over the last decade.[3]

In 1990, breast augmentation was the second-most frequently performed cosmetic surgery procedure—the first was liposuction.[3]

Over 1 million American women have had chemical sacs planted in their breasts, and the profits in the industry are between $168 million and $374 million.[4]

There are approximately 159,300 cosmetic breast operations a year.[3]

There are approximately 67,000 face-lifts a year.[3]

30,000 American women underwent the procedure of liposuction in 1991, and surgeons sucked 200,000 lbs. of body tissue from them.[5]

50,000 women had intestinal bypass surgery (in which the intestines are sealed off for weight loss) by 1983.[2]

The mortality rate for women who have had their intestines stapled (for weight loss) is 9 times above that of an identical person who forgoes surgery.[2]

Intestinal stapling causes 37 possible complications.[2]

More than 2 million women have received breast implants in the U.S.[5]

SOURCES

1. *Standard and Poor's Industry Surveys,* New York: Standard and Poor's, 1988.
2. Naomi Wolf, *The Beauty Myth,* New York: William Morrow, 1991.
3. "Breast Frenzy," *Self,* April 1989.
4. "Harper's Index," *Harper's,* January 1989.
5. *Journal of the American Medical Association,* February 12, 1992.

In a survey of women aged 18–35, 75% believed they were fat, while only 25% were medically fat.[1]

53% of high school girls are unhappy with their body by age 13; 78% are unhappy with their bodies by age 18.[2]

45% of underweight women think they are too fat.[3]

95% of enrollees in weight-loss programs are women (although the sexes are overweight in equal proportions).[4]

On any given day, 25% of women are on diets, with 50% finishing, breaking, or starting one.[3]

8 million American women are enrolled in Weight Watchers.[5]

At least 2 million Americans use diet pills.[6]

The diet industry currently grosses $33 billion a year.[7]

A California study showed that, by the time girls were in the 4th grade, 80% of them were already dieting.[2]

85% of American women diet 5 times a year; 98% regain the weight lost and then some.[2]

A generation ago, the average model weighed 8% less than the average American woman, whereas today she weighs 23% less.[8]

1 in 40,000 women meets the requirements of a model's size and shape.[2]

In one study, 99% of boys were breast-fed, but only 66% of the girls were, and they were given 50% less time to feed.[2]

In India, one of the poorest countries in the world, the very poorest women eat 1,400 calories a day, or 600 more than a Western woman on the Hilton Head Diet.[9]

90%–95% of anorexics and bulimics are women.[2]

Anorexia and bulimia strike 1 million American women a year; 30,000 also become emetic abusers.[2]

150,000 American women die of anorexia a year.[10]

Approximately 19% of hospitalized anorexics die in treatment, giving the disease one of the highest fatality rates for a mental illness.[11]

40%–50% of anorexics never recover completely, a worse rate of recovery from starvation than the 66% recovery rate for famine victims hospitalized in the war-torn Netherlands in 1944–45.[9]

Of dancers, 38% show anorexic behavior.[2]

In one survey, 50% of anorexics had been sexually abused.[2]

SOURCES

1. Drs. Wayne Wooley and Susan Wooley, University of Cincinnati College of Medicine survey, 1984.
2. Naomi Wolf, *The Beauty Myth*, New York: William Morrow, 1991.
3. Roberta Pollack Seid, *Never Too Thin: Why Women Are at War with Their Bodies*, New York: Prentice-Hall, 1989.
4. Eva Szekely, *Never Too Thin*, Toronto: The Women's Press, 1988.
5. Viv Dutch, Weight Watchers' International Statistics, September 1989.
6. "Diet Drug Ban Just a Start," *USA Today*, October 30, 1990.
7. Molly O'Neill, "Congress Looking into the Diet Business," *New York Times*, March 28, 1990.
8. Verne Palmer, "Where's the Fat?," *The Outlook*, May 13, 1987.
9. Debbie Taylor et al., *Women: A World Report*, Oxford: Oxford University Press, 1985.
10. Joan Jacobs Brumberg, *Fasting Girls: The Emergence of Anorexia as a Modern Disease*, Cambridge: Harvard University Press, 1988.
11. L. K. George Hsu, *Eating Disorders*, New York: Guildford Press, 1990.

Before the 1992 election, the United States ranked near the bottom among all the nations of the world in the percentage of women in government:[1,2,12]

>2 women out of 100 seats in the Senate (6 as of 1992)
>28 women out of 435 seats in the House (47 as of 1992)
>3 women out of 50 state governors.

After the 1992 election, the number of women in the House of Representatives rose from 28 to 47 (35 Democrats, 12 Republicans) and the number of women in the Senate rose from 2 to 6 (5 Democrats, 1 Republican).[12]

Of the voters in the 1992 election, 54% were women, and 46% were men.[13]

Total number of women who served in Congress from its inception through 1992: 134. Total number of men: 11,096.[4]

1 out of 10 federal and state judges are women.[5]

In 1991 there were 151 elected women mayors, up from 7 in 1971.[3]

The number of women in state legislatures has quadrupled in the past 20 years and is currently 18.2%.[6]

In 1991, women served in 36 of the 50 state cabinets, representing 19% of governors' appointments.[3]

Over 95% of the top female appointees in county and municipal governments were white.[3]

The fastest-growing group in American electoral politics is African-American women.[4]

In the 1990 general election, 8 women ran for the U.S. Senate and 70 women ran for the House of Representatives.[10]

In 1992, 159 women ran for seats in Congress—94 Democrats, 54 Republicans, 2 independents. Only 6 were antichoice.[7,10]

In California, 19 women running for congressional seats and 2 for the Senate triumphed in the 1992 primaries.[10]

The National Organization for Women (NOW) usually attracts about 2,000 new members a month. In the 2 months following the Anita Hill–Clarence Thomas TV spectacle, 13,000 new members signed up.[7]

Worldwide, women hold 10% of the seats in national legislatures.[9]

In one-third of governments worldwide, there are no women in the decision-making body of the country.[9]

In most countries women have attained the right to vote only in the past 30 or 40 years. Kuwait is the only country that specifically denies women the right to vote.[9]

The National Gay and Lesbian Task Force has introduced the federal gay and lesbian civil rights act to Congress, gaining 16 co-sponsors in the Senate and 104 co-sponsors in the House.[14]

The rights of lesbians and gay men are on the legislative agendas of at least 16 states in 1993.[18]

6 states have civil rights ordinances that prohibit discrimination on the basis of sexual orientation: Wisconsin, Connecticut, Massachusetts, Hawaii, New Jersey, and Vermont.[14]

26 states in the U.S. have antisodomy laws in effect; 24 states have banned antisodomy legislation.[14]

3 states—Arizona, Oregon, and Colorado—put referendums before the voters in the 1992 election which would make it legal to discriminate against gays and lesbians in jobs, housing, and other areas. Only in Colorado was the referendum passed, and massive boycotts of that state have resulted.[15,16]

One of President Clinton's first acts was to sign into law the Family and Medical Leave Act. This law, twice vetoed by President Bush, requires businesses with 50 or more employees to provide up to 12 weeks of unpaid job-protected leave to care for newborns and newly adopted children or seriously ill family members.[17]

In a poll asking people what they thought would be the effect of more women in government, 61% said things would improve, 12% said things would get worse, 14% saw no change.[8]

In response to concerns of the Vatican, the U.S. government altered its foreign-aid program to comply with the church's teachings on birth control, including an outright ban on the use of any U.S. aid funds by either countries or international health organizations for the promotion of birth control or abortion. In 1984, the U.S. withdrew funding from two of the world's largest family-planning organizations: the International Planned Parenthood Federation and the United Nations Fund for Population Activities.[11]

SOURCES

1. Sara E. Rix, ed., *The American Woman 1990–91*, New York: W. W. Norton, 1990.
2. Paula Ries and Anne J. Stone, eds., *The American Woman 1992–93*, New York: W. W. Norton, 1992.
3. "Women in Public Service," The Center for Women in Government, Rockefeller College of Public Affairs and Policy, State University of New York at Albany, 1991.
4. The Women's Political Action Group, *The Women's Voting Guide*, Berkeley: Earthworks Press, 1992.
5. Geraldine Ferraro at WAC Meeting, May 12, 1992.
6. "Women: The Road Ahead," *Time*, Special Issue, Fall 1990.
7. "Steady Local Gains by Women Fuel More Runs for High Office," *New York Times*, May 24, 1992.
8. "Nightline," ABC-TV, May 29, 1992.
9. Ruth Leger Sivard, *Women . . . A World Survey*, Washington, D.C.: World Priorties, 1985.
10. *Feminist Majority Report*, Summer 1992.
11. "The U.S. and the Vatican on Birth Control," *Time*, February 24, 1992.
12. "Democrats Promise Quick Action on Clinton Plan," *New York Times*, November 5, 1992.
13. "Portrait of the Electorate," *New York Times*, November 5, 1992.
14. The National Gay and Lesbian Task Force, Human Rights Campaign Fund.
15. "The Oregon Trail of Hate," *New York Times*, October 29, 1992.
16. The New York Boycott Colorado Organization, 1993.
17. "Clinton Signs His First Legislation," *New York Times*, February 6, 1993.
18. "Alaskan Voters to Decide on Gay Rights Ordinance," *The Times Herald Record*, April 11, 1993.

27% of Hispanics, 19.3% of African Americans, and 12.4% of whites in the U.S. have no health insurance.[1]

Seven cities have citywide domestic partnership registration and 20 cities and 5 counties have some form of health benefit plans for domestic partners.[12]

Prior to 1993, women were excluded from virtually all drug safety tests because of fear of fetal damage if they became pregnant during tests. In 1993 the FDA drafted new rules requiring researchers and drug companies to include women in all drug trials, and to carry out analysis by sex.[17]

Initial studies in over 20 countries outside the U.S. suggest RU486 as a treatment for breast cancer, for meningioma (a brain tumor that occurs twice as often in women as in men), and for Alzheimer's disease, among numerous other possible uses.[2,10]

Gay and lesbian teenagers are up to 3 times more likely to commit suicide than their heterosexual peers.[6]

Genital herpes cases increased from 15,000 in 1966 to 125,000 in 1989.[3]

By the age of 21, 1 out of 4 teenage girls is infected with a sexually transmitted disease.[3]

In 1990, 7 in 100 pregnant addicts were treated for their addiction, while 300,000 more drug-addicted babies were born. 1 in every 5 babies born in the inner cities was born addicted to drugs.[5]

The cost of drug treatment for a drug addicted mother for 9 months is $5,000. The cost of medical care for a drug-exposed baby for 20 days is $30,000.[16]

The cost of prenatal care for a pregnant woman for 9 months is $600. The cost of medical care for a premature baby for one day is $2,500.[16]

Historically, women have reported depression 3 times more often than men. Women's rate of mental health impairment fell 50%–60% between 1950 and 1980. Men's rate of depression has been found to be closely linked to their wives' employment.[7]

In 1992, an estimated 13,500 new cases of cervical cancer and 32,000 new cases of uterine cancer were diagnosed.[13]

In 1992, an estimated 4,400 deaths from cervical cancer and 5,600 from unspecified uterine cancer occurred.[13]

The death rate from uterine cancer has decreased more than 70% over the past 40 years because of PAP test detection.[13]

It is estimated that 1 in every 65 women will develop ovarian cancer by age 85.[13]

Cancer incidence and mortality rates are generally higher for African Americans than for whites. In 1989, the mortality rates were 227 per 100,000 for blacks and 169 for whites. Incidence and mortality rates for other minority groups, such as Latinos, are often lower than those for whites or African Americans.[13]

Maternal mortality rates have risen from 6.6 to 7.9 per 100,000 live births, and the rate for African-American women has increased from 14.2 to 18.4.[14]

In developing countries, cervical cancer now outranks all other cancers in women combined.[8]

Sexually transmitted diseases cause more death and illness in women than AIDS does in men, women, and children combined.[11]

Cardiovascular diseases kill 500,000 women a year. Breast cancer killed 42,200 women in 1988 and lung cancer claimed 46,400 more.[9]

One of 4 women in the U.S. smokes cigarettes.[9]

Every day, more than 1,600 teenage girls smoke for the first time.[9]

SOURCES

1. ACT UP, eds., *Women, AIDS, and Activism*, Boston: South End Press, 1990.

2. *RU486*, New York State Naral Foundation Task Force, 1992.

3. Center for Population Option, 1992.

4. Baulieu, "The Abortion Pill," *Medical Tribune*, 1992.

5. Center for Disease Control, *Medical Tribune*, 1992.

6. Hetrick-Martin Institute for Gay Youth, New York City, 1992.

7. Paula Ries and Anne J. Stone, eds., *The American Woman 1992–93*, New York: W. W. Norton, 1992.

8. Worldwatch Institute, 1992.

9. "Women Underestimate Cardiovascular Disease," *Times-Herald Record*, September 19, 1992.

10. "Foundation Presses for RU486 Research," *Feminist Majority Report*, Summer 1992.

11. Jodi L. Jacobson, "The Other Epidemic," *Worldwatch Magazine*, May 1992.

12. National Gay and Lesbian Task Force, Washington, D.C., 1992.

13. American Cancer Society, 1993.

14. "Cancer Facts and Figures—1993," American Cancer Society, Atlanta, GA, 1993.

15. "Contraceptive Use: Facts and Figures," *New York Times*, December 17, 1992.

16. Ellen L. Bessuk, "Homeless Families," *Scientific American*, December 1991.

17. "FDA Ends Ban on Women in Drug Testing," *New York Times*, March 25, 1993.

34% of the nation's homeless in 1991 were families with children (dis-proportionately single-mother families), up from 27% in 1985, and they are the fastest growing segment of America's homeless population.[1]

Each night in America, 100,000 children sleep in a shelter, on the street, or in an abandoned building.[1]

Studies estimate that between 30% and 50% of homeless children do not attend school regularly. Nearly half of homeless preschoolers manifest "serious emotional and developmental delays."[1]

89% of homeless mothers have been physically and/or sexually abused, 67% while children.[1]

Approximately 20% of homeless women have abused alcohol or drugs.[1]

40% of homeless women receive no prenatal care.[1]

Out of the average 4,000 families requiring shelter in New York City each month, at least 691, or 17%, were families with a pregnant woman or a newborn infant.[2]

55% of those in family shelters have completed high school, and 13% attended college. For single residents, 20% of men and 30% of women attended college.[2]

Between 30% and 40% of homeless and runaway teenagers are gay.[4]

The average number of children in an American family is 2.2; the average number of children in an American family on welfare is 1.9.[3]

50% of women on welfare are on welfare because the fathers of their children fail to pay child support.[2]

Since 1980 the Federal Housing Program has been cut by 80%. No new housing has been built since 1981.[3]

Average welfare grants have declined in buying power by 42% since 1970.[3]

The average amount of money for home relief is $353 per month for a single adult, $550 per month for a woman with 3 children.[2]

New York City spends an average of $2,300 per month to keep a family in a welfare hotel.[2]

SOURCES

1. Ellen L. Bessuk, "Homeless Families," *Scientific American*, December 1991.
2. Hope Sandrow, Artists and Homeless Collaborative, 1992.
3. Coalition for the Homeless, New York City, 1992.
4. Hetrick-Martin Institute for Gay Youth, New York City, 1992.

Hysterectomy is the most frequently performed major surgery in the U.S.[1]

More than a half-million hysterectomies are performed in the U.S. each year.[1,3,5]

37% of all American women will have a hysterectomy by the time they are 60 years old.[2]

Almost half of the women who have hysterectomies have surgical complications.[4]

The average age at which women get hysterectomies is 35.6 years.[1,5]

Gynecologists earned over $2.1 billion in the U.S. in 1991 just performing hysterectomies.[1]

Over 2,000 women die from hysterectomies annually.[3]

In North America a hysterectomy is performed about once every 30 seconds.[3]

More than 90% of hysterectomies are elective.[3]

In 1975, the American College of Obstetrician Gynecologists estimated that 20% of hysterectomies were performed solely for sterilization purposes.[3]

SOURCES
1. HERS (Hysterectomy Educational Resources and Services) Foundation, flyer, 1992.
2. Letter from the National Women's Health Network with statistics as reported by the National Center for Health Statistics, December 1987.
3. Herbert A. Goldfarb, The No-Hysterectomy Option, New York: John Wiley & Sons, 1990.
4. Boston Women's Health Book Collective, ed., The New Our Bodies, Ourselves, Boston: Simon & Schuster, 1992.
5. National Hospital Discharge Survey, U.S. Department of Health and Human Resources, Centers for Disease Control, 1990.

The unpaid labor of women in the household, if given economic value, would add an estimated one-third, or $4,000,000,000,000, to the world's annual economic product.[1]

In Sweden women's wages are 90% of men's; in Japan they are 43% of men's.[1]

Rural women account for more than half the food produced in the Third World and as much as 80% of food production in Africa.[1]

In Eastern Europe and the former USSR, the ratio of women to men in the paid labor force is 9 to 10. In the Middle East it is 3 to 10.[1]

In developing countries, two-thirds of the women over the age of 25 (as compared to about half the men) have never been to school.[1]

In the global community (excluding China), there are 130 million more adult women than men who cannot read or write.[1]

Women are the sole breadwinners in one-fourth to one-third of the families in the world.[1]

A survey done in Santiago, Chile, indicates that 80% of women have suffered physical, emotional, or sexual abuse by a male partner or relative; 63% report that they are currently being abused.[2]

One study of amniocentesis in a large Bombay hospital found that 95.5% of fetuses identified as female were aborted.[2]

In Bangladesh 50% of all murders are murders of wives by husbands.[2]

33% of women who come to hospital emergency rooms in Peru are victims of domestic violence.[2]

In 1990 the police officially recorded 4,835 dowry deaths in India.[3]

Because of less food and medical care, girls aged 2 to 4 die at nearly twice the rate as boys in rural Punjab, India.[2]

Doctors in Sudan have estimated that in areas where antibiotics are not available, approximately one-third of all girls die due to female circumcision, especially infibulation (vaginal stitching).[2]

In one study of 33 Somali women who had undergone sexual surgery, all had to have extensive episiotomies (cutting) during childbirth, and their second stage labor was five times longer than normal; five of their babies died, and 21 suffered oxygen deprivation due to the long and obstructed labor.[2]

According to the World Health Organization, more than 84 million women alive today have undergone sexual surgery in Africa alone.[3]

A study from Sierra Leone found that 83% of all women circumcised required medical attention sometime in their life for problems related to the procedure.[3]

In one study of 109 households in an Indian village, 22% of higher-caste husbands and 75% of lower-caste husbands admitted to beating their wives. The lower-caste wives reported that they were "regularly beaten."[3]

A study, using children as informants, reported that 57% of wives in San Salvador were beaten by their husbands.[3]

It is estimated that 75% of the world's 18 million refugees are female.[3]

Brazil has 84 all-female police stations to assist victims of violence.[3]

At a recent 12-country workshop held in China on women's nonformal education, participants were asked to name the worst aspect of being female: fear of male violence was the almost unanimous answer.[3]

50% of Ethiopian women in Somalia are widows; most of the other 50% are not with their husbands.[8]

75% of the 15 million refugees awaiting settlement are widows.[8]

Worldwide, there are 80 million more boys than girls in primary and secondary school.[1]

In India and Bangladesh, female mortality between ages 1 and 5 is 30%–50% higher than male.[1]

In China, an estimated 250,000 baby girls may have been killed since the inauguration in 1979 of a policy of 1 child per family.[1]

In rural Bangladesh, malnutrition was found to be 3 times more common among girls than among boys.[4]

United Nations High Commission on Refugees data on violence against Vietnamese boat people indicate that 39% of women are abducted and/or raped by pirates while at sea.[5]

Since 1957, because of international contraceptive programs, the total fertility rate for the developing countries, that is, the average number of children per family, has dropped from 6.1 to 3.9[6]

According to the World Health Organization, 99% of maternity-related deaths occur in developing countries.[7]

As many as 60% of women in Mexico who seek state-sponsored birth control do so without the knowledge of their spouses, because of the belief among men that contraceptive use will diminish their manhood or lead to infidelity.[9]

Throughout Sub-Saharan Africa, traditional healers promote the idea that men infected with sexually transmitted diseases should have sex with virgins to cure themselves.[9]

It is estimated that between 20,000 and 50,000 Moslem women in the former Yugoslavia have been raped, often daily for a period of months, and sometimes deliberately impregnated in the name of "ethnic purity."[10]

SOURCES

1. Ruth Leger Sivard, *Women . . . A World Survey*, Washington, D.C.: World Priorities, 1985.
2. Lori Heise, "Gender Violence as a Health Issue," fact sheet from the Violence Health and Development Project, Center for Women's Global Leadership, Rutgers University, 1992.
3. Lori Heise, "Violence Against Women: The Missing Agenda," *Women's Health: A Global View*, Westview Press, 1992.
4. S. Bhatia, "Status and Survival," World Health Organization, 1985.
5. Richard Mollica and Linda Son, "Cultural Dimensions in the Evaluation and Treatment of Sexual Trauma: An Overview," *Psychiatric Clinics of North America* 12(2): 363–379, 1989.
6. Pathfinder International Pathways in Family Planning, 1992.
7. World Health Organization, Geneva, 1986.
8. Refugee Women in Development brochure, 1992.
9. Jodi L. Jacobson, "The Other Epidemic," *Worldwatch Magazine*, May/June 1992.
10. "All Things Considered," National Public Radio, March 13, 1993.

The White House full-time press corps is 69% male, 31% female, 95% white, and 5% people of color.[1]

In the news business, women make up 44% of the country's professional work force; people of color account for 10%.[1]

The number of women in top newsroom jobs has more than tripled since 1977 to 157.[2]

In 1991 there were 2 newspapers with circulation of more than 250,000 run by women.[2]

The references to women on the front pages of 10 major and 10 small-market newspapers around the country averaged 13% during the month of February 1992.[3]

In a February 1992 survey of 10 major and 10 small-market newspapers around the country, 13% of the front-page stories contained references to women; 34% of bylines were female; 32% of front-page photographs featured women; and 13% of those solicited for comment were women.[11]

The lowest average percentage of references to women on the front pages (8%) was found in the *New York Times* and the *Los Angeles Times.*[11]

On television coverage, women reported 14% of the month's news stories, and men were sought for commentary 79% of the time.[3]

Women news anchors are 20 years younger than male news anchors and get paid 23% less.[3]

Women TV news directors earn 34% less than male counterparts.[4]

91% of voice-overs on television commercials are male.[5]

In 1990, 70% of all film roles went to men, and only 9% of all film and TV roles went to women age 40 or over.[6]

Of the 49,088 roles cast in Screen Actors Guild (SAG) film and TV projects in 1989, the largest number (41.1%) were male supporting roles. The smallest number (13.9%) were female leading roles.[10]

Women represent 43% of SAG's membership but earn 32% of SAG earnings for feature films, television, commercials, and industrial work. In 1989 men earned $644 million, women earned $296 million.[6]

Of the National Association of Radio Talkshow Hosts' 900 members, 50 are women.[7]

The median salary for female advertising managers in the corporate sector is $32,000; for their male counterparts, $45,000.[8]

The percentage of days worked by Director's Guild of America (DGA) women directors rose from 3% in 1983 to 8% in 1991.[9]

The percentage of days worked by women unit production managers rose from 5% in 1983 to 14% in 1991.[9]

The percentage of days worked by women assistant directors rose from 7% in 1983 to 14% in 1991.[9]

Women second-assistant directors worked 22% of the total number of days in 1983 and 36% in 1991.[9]

DGA minority directors' work loads declined from 5% of total days in 1983 to 3% in 1991.[9]

1991 DGA MEMBERSHIP:[9]	Total	Women	African-American	Hispanic
Director	5,478	543	109	69
Unit Prod. Mgr.	938	139	5	14
1st Asst. Dir.	852	206	24	19
2nd Asst. Dir.	659	254	25	18
Assoc. Dir.	1,194	465	47	28
Stage Mgr.	436	118	37	12
Tech Coord.	11	1	0	0
Prod. Assoc.	191	149	13	7

After the age of 10, men show consistently higher average annual earnings under SAG contracts than women do. The discrepancy increases with age as women's average earnings drop significantly in the 40s, 50s, and 60s while men's earnings peak in these age groups.[10]

Of the 34% of all film and TV roles that go to women, African Americans get 9.5%, Latinas get 3.1%, Asian-Pacifics get 2.6%, and American Indians are nearly off the chart with only 0.1% of all female roles.[10]

Women get a larger share of on-camera commercial roles than in any other field, with 41.4%. The commercial voice-over field is strongly dominated by men, however, with women receiving only 17% of these roles.[10]

Of all on-camera female roles in commercials, 85.3% went to Caucasians, while 87.5% of all female voice-over roles went to Caucasians.[10]

Of all SAG members with 1989 earnings in commercials, 33.2% were men under 40, 29.1% were women under 40, 26.2% were men 40 and over, and only 11.5% were women 40 and over.[10]

SOURCES

1. Stephen Hess, "All the President's Reporters," Society, March/April 1992.
2. John McCormick, "Making Women's Issues Front Page News," Working Woman, October 1991.
3. Edwin Diamond, "New-Girl Network," New York Magazine, June 10, 1991.
4. Janice Castro, "Women in Television," Channels, January 1988.
5. "The Portrayal of Men and Women in U. S. Television Commercials: A Recent Content Analysis and Trends over 15 years," Sex Roles, 1988.
6. 1990 statistics report, Screen Actors Guild.
7. Toni L. Kamins, "Women in Radio: Shut Up, Shut Out," EXTRA, Special Issue, 1992.
8. Judy Mann and Basia Hellwig, "The Truth about Salary Gaps," Working Woman, January 1988.
9. Directors Guild of America, 1992.
10. "The Female in Focus: In Whose Image?" Screen Actors Guild, 1990.
11. "The Fourth Annual Media Survey," conducted for the 1992 Women, Men and Media Project at the University of Southern California, 1992.

In the year 2020 there will be 60 million women at or through menopause.[1]

36 million women in the U.S. are currently at menopausal age.[3]

Today, most women live one-third of their lives after menopause.[2]

The growing market for pharmaceutical companies for hormones already exceeds $1/2 billion.[2]

At present, 15%–18% of postmenopausal women use hormone replace-ment, fewer than 1 in 5 women. Most are educated, upper middle class, and white. If doctors and manufacturers prevail, 90% of women will take replacement hormones for 3–5 decades.[1,2]

5%–15% of women have menopausal symptoms severe enough to prompt medical attention.[2]

Estrogen affects more than 300 body functions in the female physiology.[1]

85% of menopausal women experience hot flashes, which is what prompts most women to take estrogen replacement (which is 100% effective in treating it).[2]

Without estrogen treatment, women's coronary mortality rate rises 30 times within 15–20 years of menopause.[2]

With estrogen treatment, the risk of dying of heart attack may be reduced 50%.[2]

Women who take estrogen replacement sustain 40% fewer hip fractures (which result in fatal complications in 15%–20% of elderly women who suffer them).[2]

After 15 years of taking estrogen after menopause, women had a 30% increased risk for breast cancer.[2]

The risk of dying of breast cancer is 2.8% in white women 50–94 years old; the risk of dying of heart attack is 31%.[2]

A woman is 7 times more likely to develop uterine cancer after taking estrogen for more than 5 years. Both breast and uterine cancers are usually slow growing and curable.[2]

At menopause, women's calcium requirements increase from between 500 and 600 mgs a day to between 1,200 and 1,500 mgs a day. The principal metabolic cause of osteoporosis (loss of bone density) is malabsorption of calcium.[4]

50% of all women have osteoporosis by age 70, and 100% have it by age 90.[4]

Each year approximately 200,000 women suffer bone fractures that are directly attributable to osteoporosis, and 40,000 of them die of fracture complications.[4]

Before age 65, about 5% of postmenopausal women have fractures caused by osteoporosis. By age 90, the incidence of fractures in the hip is 32% and in the vertebrae about 50%.[4]

30% of all women will suffer at least one hip fracture by age 90. Hip fractures result in a 12% decrease in life expectancy.[4]

Osteoporosis affects different population groups in different ways. In the U.S. one of the most severely affected groups is white menopausal women who are small-boned and thin and who smoke. African-American women are at lowest risk because they have a greater bone density than whites. Obese women rarely develop osteoporosis.[4]

SOURCES

1. Melinda Beck et al., "The Search for Straight Talk and Safe Treatment," Newsweek, May 25, 1992.
2. Jane E. Brody, "Can Drugs Treat Menopause? Amid Doubt, Women Must Decide," New York Times, May 19, 1992.
3. "Prime Time Live," ABC-TV, October 1, 1992.
4. Margot Joan Fromer, Osteoporosis, New York: Simon & Schuster, 1986.

In 1970, 1 in 10 families were headed by women. In 1989, 1 out of 5 families were headed by women.[1]

One-third of families headed by women live below the poverty line, which was $13,359 for a family of 4 in 1990.[1]

While African-American women comprise 19% of the single women in this country, 59% of all single mothers are African American.[2]

57% of all children in female-headed households live below the poverty level.[1]

In the U.S., fathers currently owe mothers $24 billion in unpaid child support.[11]

79% of African-American children in female-headed households live below the poverty level.[1]

Of the 4.6 million Hispanic families in the U.S. in 1988, 1 million were headed by women.[2]

The high school graduation rate for female householders below the poverty level was 42.4% for Latinas, 47.9% for African Americans, and 55.2% for whites.[2]

85% of employed African-American mothers worked full time as compared with 78% of Latina mothers and 70% of white mothers.[2]

Federal funding for maternal and child health care has decreased 23.4% in the past 10 years.[3]

26% of women of childbearing age do not have health insurance that covers maternity care.[3]

One-third of teenage mothers receive inadequate prenatal care, a level about twice that of all mothers.[12]

50% of African-American mothers have no or inadequate prenatal care.[2]

During the 1980s the number of mothers receiving prenatal care declined by 2.5% annually.[5]

25% of all children—19% of white children, 30% of Latina children, 55% of African-American children—live with just 1 parent (overwhelmingly the mother).[1]

13% of white families, 44% of African-American families, and 23% of Latino families are headed by a woman.[1]

The U.S. ranks 20th out of 21 industrialized countries for infant mortality. Only South Africa—the only other First-World country without any form of socialized medicine—surpasses it.[6]

The infant mortality rate for whites is 8.5 deaths per thousand; for African Americans it is 17.6 per thousand.[7]

The maternal mortality rate for whites is 5.9 deaths per thousand; for African Americans it is 19.5 per thousand.[7]

The leading causes of early infant death are ailments easily prevented or treated by basic health care.[4]

The number of married working mothers rose from 48% in 1975 to 66% in 1988.[5]

51% of mothers of newborns return to work within the first year.[8]

By 1995, three-quarters of school age children will have working mothers.[8]

53% of mothers with children under age 6 are in the workforce.[7]

Of the nation's 6 million employers, 5,600 provided some form of child-care assistance in 1992.[6]

Less than 2% of private-sector companies and 9% of government agencies offer employer-sponsored daycare.[9]

About 34 million Americans are not covered by any insurance, including 10.6 million women and 11 million children.[5]

Approximately 10,000 children in the U.S. are being raised by lesbians who conceived through artificial insemination.[10]

Over 200 second-parent adoptions have been granted in 7 states and the District of Columbia.[10]

Approximately 3.5 million lesbian and gay Americans have had children.[10]

The states of Florida and New Hampshire have enacted laws prohibiting lesbians from adopting children.[10]

The typical woman can expect to spend 17 years caring for children and 18 years caring for older family members. 9 out of 10 women will be caregivers for either children or parents, or both.[1]

10%–17% of all births in developed countries are outside of marriage.[6]

Financial advisers recommend spending no more than 10% of family income on child care, but low-income families typically spend 20%–26%. Families with incomes of $50,000 pay less than 5%.[5]

Under the Reagan administration, federal funding for child care was cut in half. Today it remains below 1981 levels, but there are 12% more mothers in the workforce with children under age 6.[6]

SOURCES

1. Sara E. Rix, ed., *The American Woman 1990–91*, New York: W. W. Norton, 1990.
2. U.S. Department of Labor Women's Bureau, 1991.
3. WHAM! Women's Health Action Mobilization handout, 1992.

4. Susan Faludi, *Backlash*, New York: Crown Publishers, 1991.

5. Karen DeWitt, "Bigger Business Role Urged in Prenatal and Maternal Care," *New York Times*, May 1, 1992.

6. The Women's Political Action Group, *Women's Voting Guide*, Berkeley: Earthworks Press, 1992.

7. Statistical Abstracts of the United States, 1991.

8. "Women: The Road Ahead," *Time*, Special Issue, Fall 1990.

9. Paula Ries and Anne J. Stone, eds., *The American Woman 1992–93*, New York: W. W. Norton, 1992.

10. National Gay and Lesbian Task Force, Washington, D.C., 1992.

11. Report of the Federal Office of Child Support Enforcement, 1990.

12. Alan Guttmacher Institute, "Facts in Brief—Pregnancy and Birth," 1992.

In 1980, the U.S. Bureau of the Census officially stopped defining the head of household as the husband.[1]

In 1990 there were approximately 120 million males and 127 million females in the U.S.[2]

Men constitute the majority until age 35; after this, the older the age group, the higher the proportion of women.[2]

10% of American women are lesbians.[3]

The only acknowledged study about sexual preference in women dates from 1953. It found that, from puberty to age 20, 17% of girls had one or more homosexual experiences. During adulthood, 37% of Americans have homosexual experiences.[6]

Worldwide, the life expectancy of the average female born today is 66, 13 years longer than it was in 1950. In North America, female life expectancy rose from 72 in 1950 to 78 in 1985. In Africa, female life expectancy rose from 39 in 1950 to 55 in 1985.[5]

Women live 4 years longer than men, 7 years longer in developed countries, and 2 years longer in developing countries.[5]

On the average, 3.8 children are born to a woman in developing countries, 2.0 in developed.[5]

In 1990, 42% of women over 65 and 16% of men over 65 lived alone.[2]

2 of every 5 African-American women over 65 live in poverty.[2]

The median income of a married-couple family where both partners work is nearly three times that of a family headed by a woman with no spouse ($45,266 vs. $16,442).[2]

The proportion of women over 65 living in poverty is nearly double that of men.[2]

In 1988, 7,045,000 women and 5,998,000 men enrolled in college. 10% of the women were African American and 6% were Latina.[2]

As of 1987, 26% of white women and 13% of African American and Latina women had completed at least four years of college.[2]

One out of ten 15–19-year-old females gets pregnant each year.[4]

SOURCES

1. Sara E. Rix, ed., *The American Woman 1990–91*, New York: W. W. Norton, 1990.
2. Paula Ries and Anne J. Stone, eds., *The American Woman 1992–93*, New York: W. W. Norton, 1992.
3. National Gay and Lesbian Task Force, New York City, 1992.
4. Children's Defense Fund, Washington, D.C., 1991.
5. Ruth Leger Sivard, *Women . . . A World Survey*, Washington, D.C.: World Priorities, 1985.
6. A. C. Kinsey, W. B. Pomeroy, and C. E. Martin, *Sexual Behavior in the Human Female*, 1953.

In the past decade, the female prison population has grown by 202%, the male by 112%.[1]

There are 17 times more men than women in prison.[3]

73% of women in prison are under 30 years of age.[2]

66% of women in prison were unemployed before incarceration.[2]

92% of women in prison had less than a $10,000 yearly income.[2]

58% of women in prison have less than a 12th-grade education.[2]

54% of women in prison are women of color.[2]

Over 80% of women in prison are mothers.[2]

1 in 4 women entering prison is pregnant or has recently given birth.[3]

The percentage of women who give birth while in prison has been estimated at 9%. However, the thousands of statistics published by the U.S. Department of Justice include no information on prison births.[9]

New York is the only state that allows infants to stay in a prison nursery with their mothers.[9]

In the U.S. there are 48,000 women in state and federal prisons and another 42,000 in city and county jails, totaling 90,000 women in prison.[8]

The imprisonment of women has left an estimated 167,000 children without mothers.[8]

Women in prisons and jails are diagnosed with HIV infection at twice the rate of their male counterparts.[10]

Of the women incarcerated in New York, 80% are mothers, 80% have substance abuse problems, 30% are homeless, and over 25% are HIV positive.[10]

Doctors are available to women in prison 2 days a week versus 5 days a week for men.[2]

5%–10% of women in prison have VD or gynecological problems, though there are no gynecologists available for female inmates.[2]

The federal prison system's only hospital for women, in Lexington, Kentucky, does not employ a full-time obstetrician-gynecologist.[3]

Mood-altering drugs are prescribed 2–3 times more often for women in prison than for men.[2]

Prison terms for killing husbands is twice as long as for killing wives.[6]

60% of all women in federal prisons have been convicted of drug-related offenses. Estimates of the number that are indirectly drug related are 95%.[3]

64% of women in prison are drug users, and 68% of these used drugs daily before incarceration.[2]

One study found that 93% of the women who had killed their mates had been battered by them; 67% indicated the homicide resulted from an attempt to protect themselves and their children.[2]

Of 2,589 death-row inmates in the U.S., 41 are women, and over a third of the women are lesbians.[7]

10% of street gangs are girls; there are an estimated 7,000 girl gang members in the U.S.[5]

Persons arrested in the U.S., 1988:[4]

	Male	Female
Forcible rape	99%	1%
Weapons	93%	7%
Burglary	92%	8%
Robbery	92%	8%
Drunkenness	91%	9%
Vandalism	90%	10%
Stolen property	88%	12%
Vagrancy	88%	12%
Murder, manslaughter	88%	12%
Aggravated assault	87%	13%
Arson	87%	13%
Drug abuse violations	85%	15%
Offenses against family	83%	17%
Forgery	66%	34%
Embezzlement	62%	38%
Fraud	55%	45%
Runaways	44%	56%
Prostitution	35%	65%

SOURCES

1. "An Unequal Justice," *New York Times*, July 10, 1992.
2. National Coalition for Jail Reform, Washington, D.C.
3. "Women: The Road Ahead," *Time*, Special Issue, Fall 1990.
4. U.S. Department of Justice Bureau of Statistics, 1988.
5. Anne Campbell, "The Girl in the Gang," cited in June Stephenson, *Men Are Not Cost Effective: Male Crime in America*, Diemer Smith Publishing, 1991.
6. "20/20," ABC-TV, August 4, 1992.
7. "Dykes on Death Row," *Village Voice*, October 5, 1992.
8. "U.S. Prisons Challenged by Women behind Bars," *New York Times*, November 30, 1992.
9. Jean Harris, "The Babies of Bedford," *New York Times Magazine*, March 28, 1993.
10. "Hoppier Home," Women's Prison Association, New York, 1992.

In the U.S. it is estimated that a woman is raped every 1.3 minutes.[1]

1 out of every 3 women will be the victim of sexual assault during her lifetime.[2]

75% of rape victims know their attacker.[1,5]

71% of rapes are planned beforehand.[2,3]

It is estimated that 85% of rapes are never reported to the police and that less than 5% of the rapists go to jail.[1,2,3]

67% of convicted rapists are repeat offenders.[2]

The majority of rape cases occur during childhood and adolescence. 61% of all rapes occurred when the victim was 17 years old or less; 29% when the victim was less than 11 years old; 6% when the victim was older than 29.[1]

In one survey 51% of college men said they would rape if they were certain they could get away with it.[4]

The U.S. rape rate is 4 times that of Germany, 13 times as much as England, and 20 times as much as Japan.[5]

Reported rape survivors have been as old as 96 years and as young as 3 months.[2]

68% of rapes occur at night from 6 P.M. to 6 A.M.[2]

More rapes take place in the summer than in any other time of the year.[2]

More than 1 in every 7 women who have ever been married have been raped in marriage.[7]

Marital rape is legal in 2 states: North Carolina and Oklahoma.[6]

In a *Ms.* magazine survey from 1988, 42% of the rape victims told no one about their assault.[8]

1 out of 8 Hollywood movies depicts a rape theme. By the age of 18, the average youth has watched 250,000 acts of violence and 40,000 attempted murders on TV.[4,5]

In a national survey more than 70% of rape victims said they were concerned about their families discovering that they were raped, and 65% said they were worried they might be blamed for being raped.[1]

According to 1989 Justice Department statistics, in more than 75% of rapes the rapist and rape survivor belong to the same race.[5]

Rape victims are 9 times more likely than nonvictims to have attempted suicide.[8]

In a study of teenagers' attitudes, 42% of females and 51% of males feel it is okay to force sex if "she gets him excited."[6]

41% of the raped women expected to be raped again.[9]

41% of rape victims in one study were virgins.[9]

21%–30% of college women report violence from their dating partner.[9]

SOURCES

1. "Rape in America, A Report to the Nation," prepared by the National Victim Center and Crime Victims Research and Treatment Center, 1992.
2. Rape Crisis Center flyer, Washington, D.C., 1992.
3. Shelagh Marie Lafferty, "Policy Analysis Exercise, Analysis of Newspaper Coverage of Rape 1989–1990," Cambridge: Harvard University, Kennedy School of Government, 1991.
4. Caputi, Russell et al., "Violence Against Women: A Report on Life in Our Times," *Ms. Magazine,* September/October 1990.
5. "The Mind of the Rapist," *Newsweek,* July 1990, quoting U.S. Bureau of Justice Statistics.
6. National Clearinghouse on Marital and Date Rape flyer, Berkeley, California, and "The Myths About Acquaintance Rape" (n.d.).
7. Diana Russell, *Rape in Marriage,* Bloomington: Indiana University Press, 1990.
8. Lori Heise, "Violence Against Women: The Missing Agenda," *Women's Health: A Global View,* Westview Press, 1992.
9. Naomi Wolf, *The Beauty Myth,* New York: William Morrow, 1991.

In 1949, the United Nations passed a convention paper that called for the decriminalization of prostitution and the enforcement of laws against those who exploit women and children in prostitution. The paper, which was read to the United Nations General Assembly by Eleanor Roosevelt, has been ratified by more than 50 countries, but not the United States.[1]

The average age of entry into prostitution is 13.[1]

In 1983, 3,300 people under the age of 18 were arrested for prostitution.[1]

Juvenile street prostitutes see an average of 300 customers a year. Adult street prostitutes see an average of 1,500 customers a year.[1]

There are approximately 500,000 adolescent prostitutes in this country.[1]

Juvenile prostitution accounts for abut 150 million cases of sexual abuse which go undetected in this country.[1]

Runaways who end up as streetwalkers are not expected to live more than 3 years.[1]

50% of adult prostitutes are either physically or sexually abused in childhood.[1]

40% of street prostitutes are women of color. 55% of those arrested are women of color. 85% of prostitutes sentenced to do jail time are women of color.[1]

85%–90% of arrests for prostitution are made on the street, although only 10%–20% of all prostitutes are streetworkers.[1]

In 1985, police in 16 major cities made as many arrests for prostitution as for all violent crimes combined.[2]

The average prostitute in the U.S. grosses between $100 and $200 daily.[2]

The average age of street prostitutes in New York is 30 years old.[3]

Of prostitutes,[3]
> 50% are African American
> 25% are Latina
> 25% are white
> 2 out of 3 are homeless
> 4 out of 5 are using or have used drugs
> 9 out of 10 have children
> 1 in 10 lives with her children
> 1 in 3 street prostitutes carries the AIDS virus.

SOURCES

1. Frederizue, Delacoste and Priscila Alexander, eds., *Sex, Work, Writings by Women in the Sex Industry*, Cleiss Press, 1987.
2. Carol Jacobsen, Fact Sheet on Prostitution, "Live Sex Acts," *The Portable Lower East Side*, New York, 1991.
3. Dennis Breo, "AIDS Warrior Joyce Wallace Hopes to Shelter Homeless Hookers," *Journal of the American Medical Association*, March 13, 1991.

At least 1 out of every 2 women will experience sexual harassment at some point during her academic or working life.[1]

90% of sexual harassment victims are unwilling to come forward for two primary reasons: fear of retaliation and fear of loss of privacy.[1]

85% of bias crimes against lesbians go unreported.[4]

In a 1988 *Working Woman* magazine survey, 36% of formal complaints were against an immediate supervisor; 26% were against a more powerful person.[1]

Unlike the potential damages available to victims of racial discrimination, damages for sex discrimination are capped at $50,000 for small companies and $300,000 for larger ones. In 1991 a landmark ruling by the Court of Appeals for the Ninth Circuit in California held that "the appropriate perspective for judging a hostile environment claim is that of the 'reasonable woman'" and recognized that a woman's perspective may differ substantially from a man's.[1]

Women are 9 times more likely than men to quit jobs because of sexual harassment, 5 times more likely to transfer, and 3 times more likely to lose jobs.[1]

The U.S. Merit Systems Protection Board 1987 survey estimated that during a 2-year period sexual harassment cost the government $267 million in lost productivity and turnover.[1]

2 out of 3 women surveyed in a 1990 study of sexual harassment in the military said that they have been sexually harassed.[1]

Department of Defense statistics confirm that women are 3 times more likely than men to be discharged from the military for homosexuality.[5]

A *Working Woman* analysis reported that almost 90% of the Fortune 500 companies surveyed had received sexual harassment complaints; over a third had been hit with lawsuits; nearly a fourth had been repeatedly sued.[1]

In a survey of physicians, 9% of respondents admitted to sexual contact with patients. 93% of physicians who admitted sexual contact were men. 25% said their patients had reported unwanted sexual contact with other physicians.[2]

Between 6.4% and 10% of psychiatrists report having sexual contact with patients.[3]

SOURCES

1. "Sexual Harassment: Research and Resources: A Report-in-Progress," prepared by The National Council for Research on Women, November 1991.

2. *Journal of the American Medical Association*, November 20, 1991.

3. *American Journal of Psychiatry*, February 1987.

4. New York City Gay and Lesbian Anti-Violence Project, *1991 Annual Report.*

5. "Operation Lift the Ban," Human Rights Campaign Fund, Washington, D.C., 1993.

Every 15 seconds a woman is battered in the U.S.[1,5]

Battering is the greatest single cause of injury to women in the U.S., more than by car accidents, rapes, and muggings combined.[1,5,6]

In over 95% of domestic assaults, the man is the perpetrator.[2]

Nearly one-fourth of American women will be abused by a current or former partner at some point in their lives.[11]

4 million American women a year are physically assaulted by their male partners.[7]

Over 50% of doctors interviewed for a study expressed "concern about offending their patients" as the primary reason they failed to ask questions that might uncover domestic violence.[14]

One-quarter of the violent crime in the U.S. is wife assault.[9]

The FBI estimates that only about 10% of domestic violence is reported to the police.[3]

In a national survey, 28% of married couples reported at least one instance of physical assault in their relationship.[8]

In 1 out of 6 marriages in the U.S., there is a pattern of abuse. In 96% of the cases, the violence is perpetrated by the husband.[8]

60% of battered women are beaten while they are pregnant.[2]

At least 60% of battered women are sexually abused by their partners.[2]

At least 70% of men who batter their wives sexually or physically abuse their children.[2]

Violent juvenile delinquents are 4 times more likely than other youth to come from homes in which their fathers beat their mothers.[4]

VIOLENCE

Children who witness domestic violence are 5 times more likely to become batterers or victims in their adulthood.[4]

30% of divorced adults cite physical abuse as the reason for their divorce.[4]

Each year, domestic violence costs employers $3.5 billion in employee absenteeism and millions more in increased costs for health-care benefit plans.[4]

60% of the children of battered women have also been sexually or physically abused by the batterer.[4]

In the U.S., 9 out of 10 women murdered are murdered by men, half at the hands of a male partner.[6]

1 in 4 suicide attempts by women is preceded by abuse, as are half of all suicide attempts by African-American women.[6]

Battered women are 4 to 5 times more likely than nonbattered women to require psychiatric treatment and 5 times more likely to attempt suicide.[7]

At least 8% of pregnant women in the U.S. are battered during pregnancy. Such women are twice as likely to miscarry and 4 times more likely to have low-birth-weight infants, and their infants are 40 times more likely to die in the first year.[6]

In the U.S. 4 women are killed every day by their husbands or boyfriends.[5]

Spousal killings account for 12% of all murders nationwide.[8]

Nearly one-fourth of the nation's homicide victims in 1984 were related to their assailants.[8]

9 out of 10 murdered women are murdered by men. 4 out of 5 are murdered at home.[8]

Women perpetrate less than 15% of the homicides in the U.S.[8]

More than one-third of female homicide victims are killed by their husbands or boyfriends.[8,10]

Every 11 days in the U.S. a woman is murdered by her husband, boyfriend, or live-in lover.[8]

40% of women who commit murder do so in self-defense.[8]

74% of serious assaults by women were in response to attacks by their partners.[8]

Homicides committed by women are 7 times more likely to be in self-defense than are homicides committed by men.[8]

A study of a women's prison found 40% of inmates incarcerated for murder or manslaughter had killed partners who repeatedly assaulted them. These women had sought police protection at least 5 times before resorting to homicide.[15]

There is violence in 21% of relationships.[9]

In an assault, it is the woman who gets hurt in 94%–95% of the cases.[9]

38% of women have been sexually abused by an adult relative, acquaintance, or stranger before age 18.[9]

28% of women have been seriously abused before age 14, 12% by someone in their family.[9]

In 1991, 2.7 million reports of child abuse were recorded nationally; 15% (or 404,100) were child sex abuse cases.[12]

From 1976 to 1989 reports of child abuse increased 223%.[12]

27% of women and 16% of men experienced some form of sexual abuse as children.[12]

Fewer than 20% of children are abused by strangers.[12]

The victimization of 22% of boys and 23% of girls occurs before age 8.[12]

132,000 children are sexually abused annually, based on a study in 28 states.[12]

8 million girls and 5 million boys are sexually abused before they are 18. Or, 1 in 4 girls and 1 in 8 boys before they are 18.[13]

15% of the bias crimes reported to the New York Police Department in 1991 were motivated by anti-lesbian and anti-gay hate.[16]

From 1990 to 1991 there was a 16% increase in the number of reported heterosexist hate crimes against women in New York City.[16]

SOURCES

1. "On Superbowl Sunday a Woman Will Be Beaten Every Fifteen Seconds," handout, Coalition of Battered Women's Advocates, New York, 1992.
2. "Myths and Facts about Domestic Violence" (adapted from Domestic Violence Project, Ann Arbor, Michigan), (n.d.).
3. Angela Browne and Laura Brown, "Violence at Home; Partner Violence," American Psychological Association, 1991.
4. Executive Summary, National Domestic Violence Media Campaign, (n.d.).
5. "Facts on Domestic Violence," courtesy Lynne Sowder, Y Care, Chicago (n.d.).
6. Lori Heise, "Gender Violence as Health Issue" fact sheet, Violence Health and Development Project, Center for Women's Global Leadership, Rutgers University, 1992.
7. Lori Heise, "Violence Against Women: The Missing Agenda," *Women's Health: A Global Perspective*, Westview Press, 1992.
8. "Statistics, 1988, 1989," National Clearinghouse for the Defense of Battered Women, Philadelphia.
9. Naomi Wolf, *The Beauty Myth*, New York: William Morrow, 1991.
10. Federal Bureau of Investigation, *Crime in the United States: Uniform Crime Reports*, Washington, D.C.: Government Printing Office.
11. *New York Times*, from a report released by the American Medical Association, June 17, 1992.
12. The National Resource Center on Child Sexual Abuse, Huntsville, Alabama, 1992.
13. June Stephenson, *Men Are Not Cost Effective: Male Crime in America*, Diemer Smith Publishing, 1991.
14. "AMA Issues Domestic Violence Guidelines," *Feminist Majority Report*, Summer 1992.
15. National Coalition for Jail Reform, Washington, D.C.
16. New York City Gay and Lesbian Anti-Violence Project, *1991 Annual Report*.

69% of women 18 to 64 years of age are in the labor force, compared with 88% of men. In 1950, 33% of women in this age group worked.[1]

By the year 2005, women's participation in the labor force will have risen by 26%. Latina women, Asian women, Native Americans, Alaskan natives, and Pacific Islanders will have the fastest growth—80%; African-American women's labor force growth will be 34%.[1]

Based on annual earnings, for every $1 of a man's pay, a woman could expect to earn:[1,2]

in 1955: 64¢

in 1960: 61¢

in 1992: 66¢.

Nearly 75% of full-time working women, and 37% of full-time working men, earn less than $20,000.[3]

The average salary of an African-American female college graduate in a full-time position is less than that of a white male high-school dropout.[2]

Current median weekly earnings of[4]

| a female secretary: | $341 | a male secretary: | $387 |
| a female waitress: | $194 | a male waiter: | $266. |

Occupations in which women have made substantial gains include:[2]

	1975	1988
Firefighter	0	2.1
Pilot	0	3.1
Architect	4.3	14.6
Bus driver	37.7	48.5
Computer systems analyst	14.8	29.5
Economist	13.1	35.3
Lawyer/Judge	7.1	19.5
Mail carrier	8.7	22.0
Scientist	18.6	27.4

Numbers indicate percentage of women in the field.

In 1990, 46% of working women were employed in service and administrative support jobs such as secretaries, waitresses, and health aides.[4]

The number of women firefighters in the U.S. has doubled in the last 5 years. The Boulder, Colorado, Fire Department is 19% female; Madison, Wisconsin, is 12%; San Diego, California, is 8%.[11]

Women represented fewer than 3% of mechanics and repairers and 2% of construction workers in 1988, virtually unchanged over the previous 5-year period.[1]

Women were awarded one-third of all medical degrees in 1989, up from just over 10% in the early 70s, making women 20% of all physicians.[4]

Women were awarded 40% of law degrees in 1989.[4]

In 1989, 15% of undergraduate degrees in engineering went to women, up from less than 1% in 1970.[4]

Between 1977 and 1987, the number of women graduating with Master of Divinity degrees rose 224%; the number of male recipients rose 4.6%.[5]

In a survey of 92 of this country's top corporations, it was found that women represent 37.2% of employees, 16.9% of management, and 6.6% of executive management.[6]

Minority women make up 3.3% of all women corporate officers.[7]

A poll of CEOs at Fortune 1000 companies found that over 80% acknowledged that discrimination impedes female employees' progress. 1% of them regarded remedying sex discrimination policies as a goal their personnel departments should pursue.[3]

Worldwide, women account for 66% of the students studying for advanced degrees in the humanities, education, and fine arts and 25% of the students in law, engineering, and medicine.[8]

Entry-level jobs for female business school graduates paid 12% less than entry-level jobs for male graduates.[7]

Women artists earn one-third what male artists earn.[9]

69% of the owners of graphic design firms that employ others are men. 67% of the freelancers at these firms are women.[10]

Women own 28% of all businesses and are opening new businesses 50% faster than men, at a rate of 300,000 a year.[1]

In a 1982 survey, 92.5% of female-owned businesses were owned by white women, 3.8% by African-American women, 2.1% by Latina women, and 1.6% by Asian women.[1]

In the movie *Frankie and Johnny*, Al Pacino was paid $6 million, while Michelle Pfieffer got $3 million.[1]

Female lawyers comprise 25% of all associates; only 6% of partners in law firms.[1]

13.8% of African-American women have work disabilities, compared with 7.7% of white women.[1]

3.8% of disabled women have college degrees, as opposed to 20% of nondisabled women.[1]

Disabled women workers earned 38% less than nondisabled women workers in 1987.[1]

Women represent 10% of the armed services.[2]

Wives employed full time outside the home do 70% of the housework; full-time housewives do 83%.[2]

At least 1,000 women and gay men are expelled from the military every year on the basis of sexual orientation.[12]

It costs the Pentagon $27 million every year to recruit, investigate, dismiss, and replace gay personnel in the military.[12]

Women make up 11.6% of full professors nationwide. At community colleges, where the pay is lowest, they hold 38% of faculty positions.[13]

Women received 38% of the 38,000 doctorates conferred in 1992.[13]

Women at every step of the tenure ladder still earn less than men. At Harvard, male professors earn $93,600 on average while women of equal rank earn $79,900.[13]

SOURCES

1. U.S. Department of Labor Women's Bureau, 1992.
2. Sara E. Rix, ed., *The American Woman 1990–91*, New York: W. W. Norton, 1990.
3. Susan Faludi, *Backlash*, New York: Crown Publishers, 1991.
4. Paula Ries and Anne J. Stone, eds., *The American Woman 1992–93*, New York: W. W. Norton, 1992.
5. Kenneth L. Woodward, "Feminism and the Churches," *Newsweek*, February 13, 1989.
6. "A Report on The Glass Ceiling," U.S. Department of Labor, 1991.
7. Heidrick & Struggles, *The Woman Corporate Officer*, 1986.
8. Ruth Leger Sivard, *Women . . . A World Survey*, Washington, D.C.: World Priorities, 1985.
9. Guerrilla Girls, "Conscience of the Artworld," handout.
10. American Institute of Graphic Artists (AIGA) Salary & Benefits Survey, 1992.
11. Women in the Fire Service, Madison, Wisconsin, 1992.
12. "Military's Anti-gay Rule Is Costly, A Report Says," *New York Times*, June 20, 1992.
13. *New York Teacher* 34 (12), March 3, 1993.